Surprisingly Simple:

Independent Contractor,
Sole Proprietor, and LLC Taxes
Explained in 100 Pages or Less

Surprisingly Simple:

Independent Contractor, Sole Proprietor, and LLC Taxes Explained in 100 Pages or Less

Mike Piper

Dedication

For the entrepreneurial community,
the world's most powerful creative force.
That we may put our ambition to use
making this a better world for everyone.

Table of Contents

Part Three
The Big Question: Which Structure is Right for My Business?

Introduction

First, I'd like to extend my sincere congratulations on your decision to strike out on your own. Choosing to start your own business can be a wonderful thing. Obviously, many people dream of being their own boss, of controlling their work week, of being able to make a living doing what they love. Yet only a small percentage of those people ever actually decide to go ahead and do it.

The reason, of course, is that it can be quite risky to give up the steady paycheck. The good news is that, with appropriate preparation, you can substantially minimize the financial risk involved.

- Market research can help to minimize the risk that you're making a product or service that nobody is actually going to pay for.
- Setting up some cash reserves can help minimize the risk of a slow season in your business.
- Purchasing the appropriate types of insurance helps minimize the risk of liability to vendors and clients.
- Learning about the different tax rules that you are now subject to as a sole proprietor helps minimize the risk of your business failing financially.

How Understanding Tax Law Can Minimize the Financial Risk of Starting a Business

One wonderful thing about understanding tax law is that it's one of the most immediate ways you can increase the profitability of your business. As a business owner, anytime you realize that you could be deducting something that you're already paying for, you probably just got yourself a 40% discount.

On the other hand, a lack of tax knowledge can set you up for a huge surprise at the end of the year when you have to file your taxes. In fact, as a business owner, it's now important for you to understand many more parts of the tax code than you would have to understand if you worked as an employee. And sometimes, if you misinterpret something, you're going to get whacked—not just with extra tax, but with penalties and interest as well.

Is This Book for You?

The primary purpose of this guide is to explain several Federal income tax topics that are important for sole proprietors. For reference, if you are an independent contractor, or the sole owner of an LLC (Limited Liability Company), you are a sole proprietor as far as Federal income taxes are concerned. So this guide applies to you, too.

Just in case you aren't sure if you're an independent contractor (as opposed to an employee), let's make a quick clarification. For those who aren't certain: if your annual income from your work is reported on a 1099, as opposed to a W-2, you are an independent contractor. Typical independent contractor careers include real estate agents, Mary Kay® reps (or other similar sales positions), and freelance writers or web designers.

Also, just to keep from using the same term over and over, I'll periodically use the term "business owner." If you fall into any of the above categories, you *already are* a business owner (whether you think of yourself that way or not).

The three main goals of this guide are as follows:

1) To be understandable for the average person (even one with very limited knowledge of income taxes).
2) To be short enough to be read in its entirety, as compared to most of the other small business tax books on the market, which generally come in around 300-700 pages.
3) To still manage to cover the most important tax topics for small business owners.

This book is *not* for you if:

1) Your business is a corporation or partnership.
2) You are one of *multiple* owners of your LLC.
3) You are looking for an extremely in-depth discussion of many of the more technical tax issues of small business. For example, the advantages of the Modified Accelerated Cost Recovery System (MACRS) over straight-line depreciation will not be covered in this guide.

With that out of the way, and given that you're still reading, let's move on.

PART ONE

Business Taxation 101

CHAPTER ONE

Mastering Income Tax Basics

As with any area of study, it's essential to have a good grip on the basics before trying to tackle the more advanced concepts. Tax law is no different. Before getting into the tax topics specific to self-employed taxpayers, it's important to have a solid understanding of some general tax terminology as well as a few basic tax concepts.

Deductions, Exemptions, and Credits

Note: We'll be referring to the following figure over the next few sections.

     Gross Income
-   <u>Above the line deductions</u>
=   Adjusted Gross Income ← "the line"
-   Exemptions
-   <u>Below the line deductions</u> (or standard deduction<u>)</u>
=   Taxable Income

Many taxpayers are confused as to the difference between deductions, exemptions, and credits. In summary, the difference is that deductions and exemptions both reduce your taxable *income*, while credits reduce your *tax*.

Deductions

Deductions generally arise from expenses that you pay. For example, a deduction is allowed for contributing to a traditional IRA. Let's say a taxpayer is in the 25% tax bracket, and she contributes $1,000 to her traditional IRA. She will be allowed to deduct $1,000 from her taxable income, thus saving her $250 on taxes this year.

Itemized Deductions vs. Standard Deduction

Many different deductions (such as charitable contributions or the interest on your home mortgage) fall into the category known as "itemized" deductions. Sometimes, these are known as "below the line" deductions (more on that in the next section). Every year, each taxpayer has the choice to take either:

1. the sum of all of their itemized deductions, or
2. the standard deduction ($5,350 for a single taxpayer in 2007, or $10,700 for a married couple).

For the most part, this decision is pretty easy. Simply add up all of your itemized deductions, and compare it to the standard deduction you would be allowed. Then simply take whichever option allows you a larger deduction.

Above the Line vs. Below the Line Deductions

Usually, if a deduction does not fall into the category of itemized, or "below the line," it must be what is known as an "above the line" deduction. Above the line deductions are particularly valuable because a taxpayer is allowed to claim them even in years in which the taxpayer is opting to take the standard deduction.

To put it differently, below the line/itemized deductions are only valuable to the extent that they (in total) exceed your standard deduction amount. Above the line deductions, however, are valuable no matter their size and regardless of whether the taxpayer is choosing to itemize or not. Some common above the line deductions for self-employed taxpayers include contributions to a traditional IRA, contributions to a SEP IRA, and the deduction for one-half of your self-employment tax (more on each of these topics later).

To illustrate the difference between above and below the line deductions, let's use an example. John is a single taxpayer (and thus his standard deduction is $5,350). His gross income is $30,000, and his only deductions are for a $1,000 contribution to his traditional IRA (an above the line deduction) and a $500 donation to the Red Cross (a below the line deduction).

Because the IRA contribution is an above the line deduction, he will get to use it to reduce his taxable income regardless of whether he uses his standard deduction or his itemized deductions. Unfortunately, John will get no tax benefit from the charitable contribution. It is a below the line/itemized deduction. Because his itemized deductions only total $500, it wouldn't make any sense for him to itemize. Instead, he will take his $5,350 standard deduction.

To plug this example into our above equation would look like this:

> $30,000 Gross Income
> -$1,000 Above the line deduction (IRA contribution)
> =$29,000 Adjusted Gross Income ← "the line"
> -$3,400 Exemption (explained below)
> -$5,350 Standard deduction
> =$20,250 Taxable Income

Again, the reason the $500 charitable contribution doesn't show up in the above calculation is that John can use either his standard deduction ($5,350) *or* his itemized deductions ($500). As such, it wouldn't make any sense for him to use his itemized deductions.

Exemptions

Exemptions work like deductions in that they reduce your taxable income. However, they don't arise from expenses; they are simply the result of tax breaks granted by the government. For 2007, each person is entitled to an exemption of $3,400 for themselves and one for each of their dependents. For example, if a married couple has three children, whom they claim as dependents, the couple will be allowed 5 exemptions. As such, $17,000 of income would be exempt from taxes. If they are in the 25% tax bracket, this would save them $4,250 this year.

Credits

Unlike deductions and exemptions, credits reduce your taxes directly, dollar for dollar. After determining the total amount of tax you owe, you then subtract the dollar value of the credits for which you are eligible. This makes credits particularly valuable.

Credits arise from a number of things. Most often, though, they are the result of the taxpayer doing something that Congress has decided is beneficial for the community. For example, a taxpayer is allowed a credit of up to $1,650 for paying "qualified education expenses" for one of her dependents. If the taxpayer meets the requirements to claim the maximum credit, her *tax* (not taxable income) will be reduced by $1,650.

Chapter 1 Simple Summary

- Deductions generally arise from expenses that you pay. Deductions reduce your taxable income.

- Every year, you can choose to use *either* the standard deduction or the sum of all your itemized (below the line) deductions.

- Regardless of whether or not you choose to itemize, you can still use all of your above the line deductions. This makes above the line deductions particularly valuable.

- You are entitled to one exemption for you, one for your spouse, and one for each of your dependents. Each exemption you get reduces your taxable income by $3,400.

- Credits, in contrast to deductions and exemptions, reduce your tax directly (as opposed to reducing your taxable income). As such, a credit is always more valuable than a deduction of the same amount.

CHAPTER TWO

The Self-Employment Tax

One unpleasant aspect of being self-employed is paying the self-employment tax. In summary, the self-employment tax (SE tax) is a tax that gets added to your normal income tax. The SE tax is calculated by multiplying your earnings from self-employment by approximately 15%.

The Reason the Self-Employment Tax Exists

At first glance, it seems unfair that entrepreneurs—arguably the most important driving force behind our economy—would be forced to pay an additional tax. In reality, however, sole proprietors are simply paying this particular tax *instead* of another one.

If you've had a job where you were paid a salary or an hourly wage, you're probably familiar with the concept of part of your income being withheld for taxes. A portion of the amount withheld from an employee's wages goes to pay the social security and Medicare taxes.

When these taxes were originally created, Congress decided that the burden would be shared equally between the employer and the employee. These taxes are calculated as 6.2% and 1.45% of the employee's wages. At the same time, employers are also paying social security and Medicare taxes for their employees. These taxes are calculated at the same rate as the amount that the employee is responsible for. As such, an amount equal to 12.4% (or 6.2% + 6.2%) is paid in total for social security tax, and an amount equal to 2.9% (or 1.45% + 1.45%) is paid in total for Medicare taxes.

Given that you are self-employed, you are both the employee and the employer. As such, you are responsible for paying *both* halves of the social security and Medicare taxes, or 15.3% in total. We simply call the tax something different; we call it the Self-Employment Tax.

How to Calculate Your Self-Employment Tax

As long as your earnings from self-employment are $400 or more, you will be responsible for paying the SE tax. Your earnings from self-employment basically consist of exactly what you'd think: your business revenues minus your business expenses. The tax is calculated as 15.3% of your earnings from self-employment.

However, the social security portion of the tax only applies to the first $97,500 of self-employment earnings. (This number is updated annually, so be sure to check what the most recent number is.) As such, for any self-employment earnings beyond $97,500, the self-employment tax is only 2.9% rather than the usual 15.3%.

The Importance of Business Expenses (a.k.a. Schedule C Deductions)

Think back to our discussion of "above the line" vs. "below the line" deductions. One of the wonderful things about being self-employed is that you now have an additional, extra-valuable level of deductions: business deductions. These business deductions are effectively above the "above the line" deductions. The reason business deductions are so valuable is that they reduce not only your taxable income (and as such your regular income tax), but also your earnings from self-employment, thus reducing your SE tax as well.

Incorporating this new information into our equation from before, we get this:

Business Revenues
- <u>Business Expenses</u>
= Profit from business
x <u>15.3%</u>
= SE Tax

And...

Gross Income (Profit from business plus any wages or salary)
- <u>Above the line deductions</u>
= Adjusted Gross Income ← "the line"
- Exemptions
- <u>Below the line deductions</u> (or standard deduction)
= Taxable Income
x <u>Effective Tax Rate</u>
= Income Tax

And finally...

SE Tax
+ Income Tax
- <u>Credits</u>
= Total tax you owe

From now on, whenever you learn that a particular expenditure can be deducted, it will be important for you to determine whether that expenditure counts as a personal expense, or if it can be classified as a business expense, thus saving you even more money. However, be aware that the IRS isn't usually very lenient with their definitions of what can be called a business expense. (We'll be discussing several important business deductions later.) Generally speaking, if you doubt that something could reasonably be called a business expense, it probably can't.

Deduction for One-Half of SE Tax

One small piece of good news relating to the SE tax is that you can deduct it, or rather, half of it as an above the line deduction. Don't panic. That *sounds* far more confusing than it actually is. In fact, it simply ends up being a single line on your Form 1040. Even if you're doing your own taxes, you won't end up having any trouble with this part when it actually comes time to file your return. After using Schedule SE to calculate your self-employment tax, all you have to do is simply enter one-half of your self-employment tax on line 27 of your Form 1040. See? That's not so tough.

Chapter 2 Simple Summary

- The Self-Employment tax exists simply to take the place of the social security and Medicare taxes that you and your employer would be paying if you had a job as an employee.

- Your SE tax is calculated as 15.3% of your net earnings from self-employment.

- Business deductions (sometimes called Schedule C deductions) are more valuable than either above the line or below the line deductions. This is because business deductions reduce your earnings from self-employment, thereby reducing your regular income tax *and* your SE tax.

- You will get a little bit of the money you pay for SE tax back when you file your taxes for the year. This is because you are allowed an above the line deduction equal to 50% of the amount you pay for SE tax.

CHAPTER THREE

Estimated Taxes

The Federal income tax is what is known as a "pay-as-you-go" tax. This means that people and businesses are required to pay taxes as they earn income throughout the year. For anybody who is an employee, this is easy. In fact, it's done automatically in the form of withholdings from employees' paychecks. However, things work differently for business owners. When your customers pay you for your products or services, there's obviously no money withheld to go toward income taxes.

The government's solution is to require you to make tax payments at quarterly intervals throughout the year, as compared to the once-per-year filings of most people (employees). These quarterly payments are known as estimated tax payments, because the amounts you are paying are based upon an estimate of your total tax liability for the year.

How to Calculate Your Estimated Taxes

Sole proprietors use Form 1040-ES in order to calculate their required estimated tax payments. Generally speaking, the amount of estimated tax you are required to pay for the year is the smaller of:

1. 90% of your tax for this year, or
2. 100% of your tax from last year.

Given the inherent difficulty in predicting what your tax liability is going to be before you know for certain what your business income will be, it's generally recommended to just make estimated tax payments based upon the "100% of last year's total tax" option. Assuming you use this option, each of your four quarterly payments will generally just be equal to 25% of the total tax you paid last year.

There is an exception for high-income taxpayers. If your 2006 income was $150,000 or greater, instead of being able to base your estimated payments on 100% of last year's total tax, you will be required to base your payments upon 110% of last year's total tax.

Self-employed taxpayers are required to make four estimated tax payments each year. The due dates are as follows:

- For the period January 1 - March 31, payment is due April 15.
- For the period April 1 - May 31, payment is due June 15.
- For the period June 1 - August 31, payment is due Sept. 15.
- For the period September 1 – December 31, payment is due January 15 of the following year.

Note that this isn't every three months exactly. Don't make the mistake of assuming it's quarterly, or you'll end up making your second payment on July 15, and it will be a month late.

Also, please be aware that this means that on April 15, not only is your annual filing for the previous year due, but your first estimated payment for the current year is due as well. For instance, on April 15, 2008, a self-employed taxpayer will be required to file her Form 1040 for 2007 as well as make her first estimated tax payment for 2008.

The one exception to these due dates is for the January 15 payment. A taxpayer can skip the January 15 payment if, by January 31, he files his Form 1040 and pays his remaining taxes for the year just completed.

Consequences of Not Making Estimated Tax Payments

It's somewhat surprising how many self-employed taxpayers don't actually make their estimated tax payments, presumably because they either don't know how to make them, or because they don't even know they're required to make them. Unfortunately for these taxpayers, making estimated tax payments isn't optional if you have self-employment income. The penalty for underpayment of taxes is usually calculated at an annual rate of 7% or 8% for the period of underpayment. The exact percentage used varies as a function of current Treasury Bill rates.

Chapter 3 Simple Summary

- In contrast to employee taxpayers who have taxes withheld from every paycheck they receive, self-employed taxpayers have nothing withheld when they receive payments from clients. Instead, self-employed taxpayers are required to make four payments of estimated taxes each year.

- Estimated tax payments for each year are due on April 15, June 15, September 15, and January 15 of the following year.

- Generally, the easiest way to avoid penalties for estimated taxes is to make each of your four payments equal to 25% of the total tax you paid last year (or 27.5% for high-income taxpayers). This will ensure that your estimated tax payments will total 100% of last year's total tax.

CHAPTER FOUR

Required Forms for Self-Employed Taxpayers

As a self-employed taxpayer, you're responsible for meeting all of the regular filing requirements for an individual, as well as filing *at least* two other schedules. (As an aside, when talking about IRS paperwork, a "schedule" is simply an attachment to a "form.") All of the forms and schedules we'll be discussing are available for download at http://www.irs.gov/formspubs/index.html.

Schedule C

The first new piece of paperwork that you'll want to become familiar with is Schedule C. This form, whether you fill it out by hand or use software to help, basically outlines your income and expenses from your business. Schedule C itself is fairly straightforward. At the top, you fill in general information about your business: its name, address, etc.

In the next section, you list your revenues. The only time this part gets complicated is when you sell a physical product and you have to determine your Cost of Goods Sold. Even then, it's usually a fairly easy calculation done using Part

III of Schedule C. For tax purposes, the cost of the products that you sell is not actually considered an expense; it is simply subtracted from your revenues, and the remaining figure is known as your Gross Income.

In the next section, you list your total business deductions by category. For most business expenditures, it's pretty obvious which line they should go on. We'll be covering several of the different deductions more thoroughly in Chapters 8-14.

One other point of note: If you meet a few specific requirements (listed below), you're allowed to file Schedule C-EZ instead of the regular Schedule C. Basically this allows you to lump all of your business expenses together on one line rather than having to break them all out by category. Schedule C-EZ cuts the process down to three simple steps: Revenues, minus expenses, equals profit. The primary requirements to be eligible for filing Schedule C-EZ are as follows. You must:

- Have business expenses of $5,000 or less,
- Have no employees,
- Have no inventory,
- Not deduct expenses for business use of your home,
- Not depreciate or Section 179 expense any property for your business,
- Have a net profit from your business.

Just as a reminder, the deductions entered on Schedule C are the "above the above the line" deductions. These are your most valuable deductions because they are subtracted from your income *before* the Self-Employment tax is calculated, thus increasing their value by 15.3% (the tax rate of the SE Tax) over other deductions. Now that you're self-employed, if you're ever trying to calculate the financial benefit provided by a given deduction, it's important to learn whether it is:

a) a Schedule C deduction,

b) an above the line deduction, or

c) a below the line deduction.

Schedule SE

Schedule SE is another form you're going to get to know pretty well. Luckily, it's not terribly complicated. This is where your Self-Employment tax gets calculated. Most business owners are allowed to file the short version of Schedule SE. After filling out Schedule C completely, Schedule SE will only take a few minutes.

Form 4562

If you use any depreciable property (such as furniture) for your business, this is the form you have to fill out to calculate your deduction. We'll be covering this topic in more detail in Chapter 11. Be aware that Form 4562 can be rather difficult. While we'll go over the general concepts of depreciation and knowing what you can deduct when, the actual how-to of filling out Form 4562 is somewhat beyond the scope of this guide. To give you an idea of its complexity: the IRS (in the 2006 version of the Instructions for Form 4562) estimates the amount of time required to fill out the form as 5 hours and 5 minutes. And that doesn't even include the estimated 4 hours and 16 minutes to learn about the tax code that applies to the form!

Form 8829

Form 8829 is the form on which you would calculate your Home Office Deduction. We'll cover this topic in depth in Chapter 13, and when we do, you'll see that this form is one that can save you a *ton* of money. In recent years, Congress has made qualifying for the Home Office Deduction much easier. That said, nobody's made filling out this form any easier. It's a monster for the average taxpayer. You're certainly capable of doing it on your own if you want to, but be sure to save several hours fill it out.

Chapter 4 Simple Summary

- Schedule C is the form on which you detail your business revenues and expenses.

- If possible (see requirements listed above), use Schedule C-EZ. It will save you lots of time.

- Schedule SE is the form on which you calculate the amount of Self-Employment tax you owe for the year.

- Form 4562 is the form you will use if you intend to deduct expenditures related to purchases of equipment for your business.

- Form 8829 is the form used to calculate your Home Office Deduction.

- Save several hours to complete Form 8829 and Form 4562 if you plan to do them yourself.

CHAPTER FIVE

Considering Tax Consequences When Making Business Decisions

Obviously one benefit of a greater knowledge of taxes is that you will likely be able to take deductions and/or credits that you may otherwise have missed. However, another less obvious benefit is that you can use your tax knowledge to figure out the true cost of expenditures you are considering as well as the real in-your-pocket income resulting from revenues you are projecting. This ability will be of tremendous value when making business decisions.

When calculating the tax consequences of an action, the first thing you need to know is your "marginal tax rate." For most taxpayers, their marginal tax rate is simply the highest tax bracket they make it to. To understand this concept, you must first understand that the federal income tax is a progressive tax. This means that that percentage of the tax increases as your taxable income increases. For a single taxpayer in 2007, your first $7,825 will be taxed at 10%, the next $24,025 at 15%, and so on upward until the highest tax bracket of 35%. The following are the 2007 tax brackets for single taxpayers and taxpayers who are married filing jointly.

Single (2007)

If taxable income is over:	But not over:	The tax is:
$0	$7,825	10% of the amount over $0
$7,825	$31,850	$782.50 plus 15% of the amount over 7,825
$31,850	$77,100	$4,386.25 plus 25% of the amount over 31,850
$77,100	$160,850	$15,698.75 plus 28% of the amount over 77,100
$160,850	$349,700	$39,148.75 plus 33% of the amount over 160,850
$349,700	no limit	$101,469.25 plus 35% of the amount over 349,700

Married Filing Jointly (2007)

If taxable income is over:	But not over:	The tax is:
$0	$15,650	10% of the amount over $0
$15,650	$63,700	$1,565.00 plus 15% of the amount over 15,650
$63,700	$128,500	$8,772.50 plus 25% of the amount over 63,700
$128,500	$195,850	$24,972.50 plus 28% of the amount over 128,500
$195,850	$349,700	$43,830.50 plus 33% of the amount over 195,850
$349,700	no limit	$94,601.00 plus 35% of the amount over 349,700

Again, for most taxpayers, their marginal tax rate is the highest tax bracket that they make it to. For instance if a single taxpayer makes $60,000, his marginal tax bracket is 25%. As a self-employed taxpayer, however, you now know that you have both business deductions and personal deductions. For personal deductions, the same analysis applies as for most taxpayers. However, for business deductions, you must remember to include the 15% for self-employment taxes. For example, if you are in the 25% bracket, your marginal tax rate will be 25% for personal deductions, and 40% for business deductions.

Real World Application

Let's say your marginal tax rate is 25% and you are weighing two expenditures against each other, both of which are expected to produce the same amount of revenue:
   1) A deductible expenditure of $8,000. An advertising campaign, let's say.
   2) A non-deductible expenditure of $7,000. An illegal bribe perhaps? Not only are they unethical and illegal (which we'll ignore for the sake of the example), but they're nondeductible too!

The true cost of a deductible expenditure is equal to the amount of the expenditure minus the tax savings from the resulting deduction. To put it mathematically:

True cost of an expenditure = Apparent cost − Tax savings

Tax savings = Amount of deduction x Marginal tax rate

Using our equations above, we can determine that the true cost of the deductible advertising expenditure is $6,000 while the true cost of the nondeductible bribe (not counting potential jail time) is $7,000. As such, the advertising is the better of the two options.

One of the most common misunderstandings of tax law is the notion that, because something is deductible, it's basically free. In other words, some people think that the tax savings from a deduction is equal to the amount of the deduction. Because you're now armed with a better understanding of the situation, you understand why this belief is completely incorrect.

Chapter 5 Simple Summary

- Your tax savings from a deduction is equal to your marginal tax rate times the amount of the deduction.

- For personal deductions, your marginal tax rate is equal to the highest tax bracket that your income falls into.

- For business deductions, your marginal tax rate is equal to your personal deduction marginal tax rate, plus 15.3% (to account for savings on your SE tax).

- An expenditure being deductible (sometimes referred to as being a "write off") does not mean that it is actually free. It simply means that you'll get some tax savings from it. (This is more or less the same as getting a discount on the expenditure.)

CHAPTER SIX

Recordkeeping

When running a business, good recordkeeping is essential. As you probably already know, keeping detailed records helps you to more accurately track how well your business is doing. Records allow you to see what expenses could likely be cut, what expenditures are producing results and should be increased, which customers are your most profitable, and so on.

Recordkeeping is also essential for tax purposes. First, it makes the job much easier for the person preparing your taxes, whether you're doing it yourself or getting professional help. You can save yourself a nightmare at tax time by keeping an organized list of your taxable receipts and deductible expenditures.

Equally important is the need to have sufficient records in case of an audit. If you're audited and cannot produce evidence of an expense you claimed as a deduction, the deduction is almost certain to be disallowed. There are several recordkeeping software products (i.e. QuickBooks®) on the market that are both affordable and fairly easy to use. The financial risk you incur by not keeping records far outweighs the cost of such software.

What Records to Keep

The first step, if you haven't done so already, is to get a business checking account. Being able to separate your business expenses from your personal expenses will prove invaluable both for evaluating your success and for doing your taxes.

The most important record to keep is a ledger. This is a record of all of your business transactions. (Your personal ledger is the little booklet that accompanies your checks in your checkbook.) You can find paper versions of these at business supply stores, but it's strongly recommended to find software to help you with this. However, if you do use a software package to help you, be sure to backup your file regularly. Losing this information due to something as simple as a computer failure would be an absolute shame.

For tax purposes, you will also be required to maintain supporting documents for your ledger. For your income items, these will be things such as invoices, bank deposit slips, and so on. (If you run a business with lots of cash sales, an important record to keep is a daily log of the amount of cash received.) For expenses, your supporting documents will be receipts, credit card statements, bank statements, invoices, etc.

How Long to Keep Your Records

For tax purposes, the general rule is that you want to keep records until the applicable "statute of limitations" runs out. The statute of limitations is the period during which a) you can amend your return to claim a refund, or b) the IRS can assess an additional tax. For the most part, this is three years after the date the return was filed or the date the return was due, whichever is later.

There are two major exceptions to this three-year period. First, if you file a fraudulent return or do not file a return, the IRS has an unlimited amount of time to assess additional tax. Second, if you do not report income that you should have reported, and it is more than 25% of your gross income for the year, the applicable statute of limitations is six years.

So for the most part, three years is the length of time required to keep records for tax purposes. However, there are several reasons you may want to keep records (at least some of them) for far longer than that. Generally you will want to keep at least your ledger of revenues and expenses (although not the actual receipts) more or less indefinitely. This information will continue to be valuable for tracking your business's progress. Also, your insurance company or creditors will quite possibly require you to maintain your records for longer than three years. Finally, your state law may require recordkeeping for longer than three years.

Chapter 6 Simple Summary

- The most important thing you can do to make filing your taxes simpler is to get a separate checking account for your business.

- In case of an audit, you want to have both a canceled check (or credit card statement) and a receipt to prove each of your claimed deductions.

- Generally, you want to make sure to keep your records for three years for tax purposes, but you may be required to keep records for longer for your bank or insurance company.

CHAPTER SEVEN

Potential Pitfall: Hobby Classification

You might be surprised to learn that, as a business owner, you actually have to prove to the IRS that you're in business to make a profit. If the IRS determines that the activity that you think of as your business is not actually a business, but a hobby, the tax consequences can be disastrous. The reason for this distinction is that the IRS does not want taxpayers to be able to engage in activities primarily for fun, and then simply call the activity a business and attempt to deduct the related expenses.

Ramifications of Your Business Being Treated as a Hobby

Should it be determined that your business is going to be treated as a hobby for tax purposes, your ability to take deductions will be severely limited. First, any deductions that you take will no longer be treated as Schedule C deductions; they will become itemized deductions (thus only benefiting you if they, along with your other itemized deductions, exceed your standard deduction).

In addition, the itemized deductions are included in the type known as "miscellaneous" itemized deductions. What this means is that they can only be deducted to the extent that they exceed 2% of your Adjusted Gross Income (basically your taxable income minus any above the line deductions).

Finally, the deductions you can take for the activity are limited to your income from the activity. As such, if you have a loss from your business/hobby, you won't be able to use it to reduce your taxable income from other sources.

How to Make Sure Your Business Isn't Ruled to Be a Hobby

Fortunately, there are several things you can do (and are probably already doing) that can help you prove to the IRS that you are in fact running a for-profit business. The most important thing you could do is to actually earn a profit. If your activity has earned a profit for three of the last five years, it is presumed to be a for-profit business.

If your activity has thus far been unprofitable, or if you just started your business, there are a number of other factors that are considered before it is declared that your business is in fact a hobby:

- How much time and effort do you put into the activity? (The more, the better.)
- Do you depend on the activity for income?
- Do you conduct the activity in a business-like manner? (Having business cards and customized letterhead, for example, will help with this.)
- Do you have the level of expertise necessary to be able to earn a profit from the activity?
- Do you regularly improve upon your processes in order to improve your profitability?

- Have you made a profit with similar activities in the past?
- Were the majority of the years with losses during the start-up phase of the business, or were the losses due to circumstances beyond your control?

Chapter 7 Simple Summary

- If the IRS declares that your business is really just a hobby, the tax consequences will be quite unfortunate. Your business deductions will suddenly become itemized deductions, and will be limited to your hobby income.

- The best thing you can do to avoid hobby classification is to earn a profit with your business.

- Even if you don't earn a profit, if you make sure to run things professionally, you're more likely to avoid hobby classification.

PART TWO

Business Deductions

CHAPTER EIGHT

Local Transportation
Expenses

While important for every business owner, this section will be particularly valuable for sales professionals in independent contractor roles (unless you've devised a brilliant plan to get your prospects to come to you instead of the other way around). The topic of local transportation is one in which proper planning can save a business owner a significant amount of money. Please note that any long distance travel or overnight travel will be discussed in the following chapter.

Commute vs. Transportation

The first thing to discuss when speaking about the deductibility of local travel expenses is the issue of commuting. Having your travel treated as "commuting" is much like having your business treated as a "hobby." It's bad news because you lose your deduction. Any trip between a person's home and her main place of work is ruled to be commuting, and is entirely nondeductible.

Local trips that you can deduct, however, include:

1) trips from one workplace to another,

2) trips to visit clients, and
3) trips from your home to a temporary work location.

A temporary work location is any work location where you expect to be working for less than one year. [Note: If you do end up working at the location for greater than one year, even if you had reason to believe that you would not, your deduction will be disallowed.]

One important fact to know is that if you have an office in your home that qualifies as your principal place of business (see Chapter 13), you can deduct your costs of transportation from that office to another workplace. Thus, by restructuring things a little so you qualify for the home office deduction (more on this later), you may likely be able to change what would otherwise be a nondeductible commute into deductible business transportation.

Actual Car Expenses vs. Standard Mileage Rate

If you use a car (or other vehicle you own) for your local business transportation, you have two options for determining the size of your deduction:
1) Your actual car expenses
2) The standard mileage rate.

If you choose to use the first method, you can deduct the price of gas, oil, repairs, depreciation, and any other ordinary and necessary expenses for operating your car. Depending upon your situation (such as what type of car you drive, how old it is, if you drive primarily on the highway or on busy streets), this deduction could quite possibly be larger than the other option. The downside is that to deduct your actual expenses, you'll need to do far more recordkeeping than if you opt for the standard mileage rate. Rather than simply keeping a log of how many miles you drive for business, you'll be required to keep gas receipts, receipts for oil changes, receipts for repairs/maintenance, etc.

The standard mileage rate method of calculating your deduction is quite simple. All you have to do is multiply the number of miles you drive for local business transportation by the current year's given amount. (The amount for 2007 is 48.5 cents per mile.) As such, all you will have to keep track of is the number of business-related miles you drive.

One important note is that if you ever want to use the standard mileage rate for your car, you must use it in the first year that you use that car for your business. If you use the standard mileage rate in the first year, you then have the option to continue to use it, or to switch to the actual expense method in any year that you want to. If you use the actual expense method in the first year, you're going to be stuck using that method for the entire time you use the vehicle.

Using Public Transportation

If you use public transportation rather than your own vehicle to do your local business traveling, you only have one option for calculating your deduction. The good news is that it's pretty straightforward. After determining which of your trips are deductible (see above) you simply add up the costs of each of those trips. It doesn't matter whether you took a train, a bus, a taxi, or any other public transportation method.

Chapter 8 Simple Summary

- The cost of commuting between your home and regular place of work is nondeductible.

- Local trips to visit clients, trips from one workplace to another, and trips from your home to a temporary work location are deductible.

- You can deduct either the actual costs of operating the vehicle, or the standard mileage rate. If you plan to deduct actual costs, you will need to keep records of all of those costs, the same way you would for any other business expenses.

- If you ever plan to use the standard mileage rate for a vehicle, be sure to use it for the first year in which you use that vehicle for business. After that, you'll be allowed to switch back and forth as you please.

CHAPTER NINE

Non-Local Travel Expenses

As a business owner, it's likely that from time to time, you will find it necessary to travel away from home for business reasons. Generally speaking, the trip qualifies as a business expense as long as

1) you are away from your tax home, and
2) the trip is ordinary and necessary for your business

For the most part, your tax home is the city or general area that includes your primary place of business. Interestingly enough, for these purposes, it does not matter where your family home is. That said, note that travel between your tax home and your family home is not business-related, and is not deductible.

Away from Home

You are "away from home" anytime you are required to either 1) stay away from your tax home for significantly longer than an ordinary work-day, or 2) need to sleep while away from your tax home in order to meet your work's demands. The IRS has consistently determined that simply napping in your car, however, does not meet requirement #2.

What's Deductible

If your trip is entirely for business purposes, all of the following costs are deductible:
1) Transportation (both to your destination as well as local travel once there)
2) Lodging
3) Dry cleaning/laundry
4) Any shipping costs for your baggage.
5) 50% of meals (covered later)
6) Any other expense which is ordinary and necessary and related to your travel.

Deductions for Meals While Traveling

When determining the amount of your deduction for meals while traveling, you have two options. Your first option is to keep track of your actual meal expenses while traveling for business. Your can then deduct 50% of the cost of those meals. The justification for only allowing you to deduct 50% of your meal expenses is that Congress assumes you would already be spending at least some money on meals even if you weren't traveling (presumably, approximately half as much).

Your second option is to use a number referred to as the "per diem rate" as a substitute for your actual meal costs. The per diem rate is a number that varies based upon the location of your travel. For 2007, the per diem rates range from $39-$64. You can find a listing of the per diem rates by city in IRS Publication 1542, available at:
http://www.irs.gov/publications/p1542/index.html.

If you use the per diem rate as a substitute for actual meal costs, you are still only allowed a 50% deduction. For example, if you were traveling for business for three days to a location with a per diem rate of $60, your deduction for meals would be calculated as:

$$(\$60 \text{ per day} \times 3 \text{ days}) \times 50\% = \$90$$

Travel Not Exclusively for Business

The above discussion applies only if you are traveling within the United States, and your trip was entirely for business. If your trip was primarily for business, and while you were there, you extended your stay for personal reasons, you can deduct only the costs of the business-related travel expenses. If your trip was primarily for personal reasons, the entire cost is nondeductible, even if you engaged in some business while on the trip.

Let's say you took a five-day trip to Florida with a friend of yours who also happens to be a client. If over the five days, you spend most of the time at the beach, your expenses will be nondeductible, even if you end up having a business conversation over lunch at one point.

If your trip is outside the United States, and is exclusively for business, the same rules apply as if it were within the U.S. (That is, the entire trip is deductible, with the exception of 50% of your meal costs.) If your trip is outside the U.S., and is primarily for business purposes, the same rule applies as above, in that you can deduct only the business-related travel expenses. However, you must also remove from your deduction a portion of the actual transportation costs. The amount of the transportation costs you are allowed to deduct is determined by allocating the transportation costs to business use and to personal use based upon the number of days spent for each purpose. For example, if your trip is 9 days long, and 6 of them are business-related, you can deduct 2/3 of your transportation costs. If your trip outside the U.S.

was primarily for personal reasons, the entire cost is nondeductible, even if you engaged in some business while on the trip.

Chapter 9 Simple Summary

- Whether traveling within the U.S. or outside the U.S., if your trip is *exclusively* for business, the majority of your related expenses will be deductible.

- When traveling *inside* the U.S., if your trip is *primarily* for business reasons, you'll be able to deduct all of the cost of transportation, as well as the business-related expenses.

- When traveling *outside* the U.S., if your trip is *primarily* for business reasons, you can deduct a portion of your transportation cost, and all of the business-related costs.

- When traveling inside the U.S. or outside the U.S., if your trip is primarily for personal reasons, it's going to be nondeductible.

- If the trip counts as a deductible trip, you will still only be able to deduct 50% of the cost of meals. You can either keep track of the actual cost of the meals, or you can use the applicable per diem rate as a substitute for the actual cost.

CHAPTER TEN

Business Start-Up Costs and Organizational Costs

As anybody who has ever started a business knows, it takes some money (sometimes a *lot* of money) to get things up and running. It seems intuitive that these expenditures should be deductible. After all, they're obviously related to your business, right? The catch here is that your business hasn't actually begun operating yet. So, by default, you can't have business-operating expenses. As such, these expenditures receive special treatment.

How Start-Up and Organizational Costs Are Normally Treated

For the most part, business start-up costs and organizational costs must be deducted over a 180-month (15 year) period. For example, if your start-up costs were $18,000, and you started your business on July 1, 2007, you would be able to deduct $600 in 2007 for your start-up costs. ($18,000 divided by 180 months = $100 per month. If started in July, the business will be operating for six months in 2007.)

Why Wait to Get Your Tax Savings?

The good news is that the tax code now allows you to deduct in your first year of operation up to $5,000 each for business start-up costs and organizational costs for a total deduction of $10,000. This basically allows you to receive the tax benefit from the deduction all at once rather than having to realize the benefit over a 15-year period.

There is one exception to be aware of, and it's a bit complicated, so don't feel bad if you have to read it twice: the amount of start-up costs or organizational costs that you can elect to deduct in your first year (normally $5,000) is reduced by the amount that your *total* start-up costs or organizational costs exceed $50,000.

Let's say you start a publishing business, and your start up costs total $53,000. As such, the total amount you can deduct in the first year is reduced by $3,000 (because $53,000 exceeds $50,000 by $3,000). Thus, instead of being able to deduct the usual $5,000 for start-up costs, you can only deduct $2,000 in your first year of operation. Your remaining $51,000 of start-up costs will have to be deducted over 180 months.

Eligible Start-Up Costs

Business start-up costs are costs paid for creating a trade or business as well as costs paid for investigating the creation or acquisition of an active trade or business. For the most part, start-up costs are the costs that, if your business were already running, would simply be your regular operational costs. Some common examples of start-up costs include:
- Advertising the opening of the business.

- Costs associated with creating a web site.
- Rent paid in advance of the opening of the business.
- Costs from analyzing potential markets, products, etc.

Eligible Organizational Costs

Organizational costs are costs incurred to create the legal structure of the business. Examples of common organizational costs include:

- State incorporation fees.
- Costs for legal advice regarding the legal structure of your business.

Nondeductible Costs

There are, however, a few nondeductible costs that many people assume would be deductible. Costs that cannot be deducted as start-up costs or as organizational costs include:

- Interest or taxes that would be deductible if the business were already in operation.
- Costs for issuing and selling stock in your business.
- Costs associated with transferring assets to the business.

Chapter 10 Simple Summary

- Unless you incur a very large amount (greater than $50,000) in organizational costs or start-up costs, you can deduct $5,000 of each in your first year of operation.

- Deductible start-up costs consist of expenditures that would be deductible as regular operating expenses if your business was already in operation. (Advertising and rent, for example.)

- Deductible organizational costs are the costs incurred to organize the legal structure of the business. (Attorney fees and state incorporation fees are primary examples.)

- If your organizational or start-up costs are sufficiently high that you are not eligible to deduct them in the first year of operation, you will have to deduct them over a 15-year period.

CHAPTER ELEVEN

Depreciation and Section 179 Election

For the most part, as long as the IRS agrees with you that a business expenditure is "ordinary and necessary," it allows you to deduct it in the year you incur the expense. One major exception to this rule is for expenditures that can be reasonably expected to provide benefit to your business for greater than one year. A common example would be the purchase of a desk for your office (whether at home or not). Obviously, the desk is going to last you for more than one year. As such, you are required to spread your deduction for the desk out over multiple years. This process is known as depreciation.

How Depreciation Usually Works

There are several methods that can be used to depreciate capital assets. ("Capital asset" is the term used for an asset that will last longer than a year.) Some of these methods are pretty straightforward, such as "straight line depreciation" in which you deduct an equal amount each year, until the entire cost of the asset has been depreciated. Other methods, such as the "Modified Accelerated Cost Recovery System," are decidedly more complex, although they allow you to receive a greater percentage of the deduction earlier in the life of the asset.

The good news is that you probably won't have to learn exactly how any of the depreciation methods work. That's because you most likely won't be using them. You'll be using the "Section 179 Election." However, if for some reason you find yourself needing more information about depreciation methods, you can find it in IRS Publication 946, available at http://www.irs.gov/publications/p946/index.html.

What's the Section 179 Election?

Under Section 179 of the Internal Revenue Code, you are allowed to expense (deduct) the entire cost of a capital asset in the first year in which you use it for business. The benefit of using Section 179 is obvious: it allows you to get money off your taxes sooner rather than later.

What's the catch? There are two. First, there are some limits as to the amount of expenditures that you can deduct in one year using Section 179. That said, most of these limits don't come into play unless you plan on placing more than $125,000 worth of capital assets into use for your business in one year. As you can see, most small business owners needn't worry. Likely, the only limit you need to worry about is as follows: Your Section 179 election amount is limited to your income from the business in which the asset is used.

The second catch is that, as the law stands right now, the ability to take this election will only last through the end of 2010. Unless Congress passes an extension, as of 2011, we'll be back to using regular depreciation. Many experts think it's very likely that Congress will extend the time frame for Section 179 (perhaps permanently), but there is really no way to know for sure. As such, if you're planning on acquiring a large amount of capital assets for use in your business, it might be a good idea to budget the costs for prior to 2011.

What Is Eligible and What Isn't

Almost any asset used for your business qualifies for Section 179. Therefore, it's easier to simply list what isn't eligible. The following cannot be expensed under Section 179:

- Property that you lease to others.
- Property used predominantly outside the United States.
- Property used predominantly to furnish lodging (for example, furniture used in the rented rooms at a Bed & Breakfast).
- Air conditioning or heating units.

Property Used Only Partially for Business

If you have an asset that you use partially for your business and partially for personal reasons, you can still deduct part of it under Section 179. As you would expect, the portion you can deduct is equal to the business use percentage for the asset. For example, if you bought furniture for your office worth $3,000, but you use it 10% of the time for personal reasons, you calculate your deduction as follows:

$3,000 x 90% (business use percentage) = $2,700 deduction

Listed Property & Ramifications

Pay attention here. This part is important, because it's an area where many self-employed taxpayers make mistakes that end up resulting in them owing more taxes than they had planned on. If an asset is categorized as "listed property," it is subject to special rules and restrictions (explained below) in terms of how it can be depreciated/expensed. The following items are listed property:

- Passenger automobiles weighing 6,000 pounds or less.
- Any other vehicle used for transportation (except for vehicles such as ambulances or police cars for which an explicit exception is made).
- Property generally used for entertainment (examples: cameras and video-recording equipment).
- Cell phones and other similar devices (i.e., Blackberries, Treos, etc.)
- Computers and peripheral equipment, unless used exclusively at a regular business establishment and owned by the person who owns the establishment. (Home offices that qualify for the deduction as discussed in Chapter 13 will satisfy this requirement.)

The most important rule regarding listed property is that if it is used 50% or less for business, it is not eligible for the Section 179 election. As such, you'll have to depreciate it over several years. (The length of time depends on the asset, and can be found in IRS Publication 946.) In fact, you will be required to use the straight line method, which is the slowest of all depreciation methods.

Even if your listed property is used more than 50% for business, you will be required to keep records (a daily log, for instance) to prove that it is used predominantly for business.

Chapter 11 Simple Summary

- If you purchase equipment to be used exclusively in your business, you can generally deduct it in the year you place it into use (using what's known as the Section 179 election).

- If the equipment is listed property (defined above) and is to be used 50% or less for business, you cannot take the Section 179 election. Instead you must deduct it over a longer period of time. (See IRS Publication 946).

- If the equipment is listed property and is to be used at least 51% for business purposes, you can use Section 179 to deduct the business-use portion of the cost. (For instance, 60% of the cost if you use the equipment for business 60% of the time.)

- If the equipment is not listed property, you can deduct the business-use percentage of the cost, regardless of whether the equipment is used primarily for business or not. (For example, even if it's used only 30% for business, you can still use Section 179 to deduct that 30% in the first year.)

CHAPTER TWELVE

Deductible Health Insurance Premiums

As we've discussed, most business expenses are deductible to the business owner in some form or another. What's unique about the topic of health insurance is that it isn't exactly a business expense, but as a self-employed taxpayer, you may be able to deduct it anyway.

Who Is Eligible and Who Isn't Eligible

If you're self-employed and you are *not* eligible for coverage under a subsidized plan provided by your employer (if you have an employer) or your spouse's employer, you can deduct certain health insurance premiums. In other words, if your spouse works somewhere that provides a subsidized insurance plan, you are not eligible for this deduction, even if you choose not to participate in the plan. Or, if your business is part-time, and you also have an employer, you aren't eligible for this deduction if your employer provides a subsidized insurance plan under which you could receive coverage.

Where to Deduct Health Insurance Premiums

Now that you are aware of the different types of deductions available to you, your next question is of course, "What type of deduction is this?" The answer is that it isn't a business deduction, but it is at least an above the line deduction. In other words, it isn't going to save you any money on your self-employment tax. However, it *is* going to be beneficial regardless of whether you choose to itemize or to take the standard deduction.

What Premiums Can be Deducted

For the most part, any health insurance and dental insurance premiums paid for yourself, your spouse, or your dependents can be deducted (assuming you're eligible in the first place). Also, you may be able to deduct premiums related to long-term care insurance (see below). In either case, your total deduction for health insurance premiums is limited to your income from your business.

Long-Term Care Insurance: Is it Deductible too?

In order to be able to deduct the premiums for long-term care insurance, the policy must be a "qualified long-term care insurance contract." In other words, it must meet all the following requirements:
- It must be guaranteed renewable.
- It must not provide any cash surrender value or other money that can be borrowed or withdrawn from the plan.

- It must not pay for items that would be covered under Medicare, except when the contract simply provides a per diem amount of coverage without regard to expenses.
- It must provide that dividends and refunds (other than refunds from the death of the insured or from cancellation of the contract) may be used only to reduce future premiums or increase future benefits.
- It must only provide coverage of qualified long-term care services. (The primary requirements for qualified long-term care services are that they must be required by a chronically ill individual and prescribed by a licensed health care practitioner.)

Also, the amount that you can deduct for long-term care premiums is limited to the lesser of the following for each person covered:

1. The total amount paid for that person for the entire year.
2. An amount based upon the person's age.
   - 40 or younger: $280
   - 41-50: $530
   - 51-60: $1,060
   - 61-70: $2,830
   - 70 and up: $3,530

Chapter 12 Simple Summary

- If you are not eligible for coverage under a subsidized plan from either your own or your spouse's employer, you are eligible for an above the line deduction for health insurance and dental insurance premiums you pay for yourself, your spouse, and your dependents.

- You may also be able to deduct premiums paid for a long-term care insurance policy if the policy meets several specific requirements (outlined above).

CHAPTER THIRTEEN

Home Office Deduction

In order to run a business, you obviously need a place to work. Over the last decade, there has been a dramatic increase in the number of business owners who choose to work out of their homes. Previously, it used to be extremely difficult to meet the stringent requirements to qualify to deduct expenses related to your home office. However, in 1999, Congress passed a law that made it significantly easier to qualify to deduct expenses related to the business use of your home.

How to Know if You're Qualified

To qualify as a home office, the area in question does not necessarily need to have a physical barrier from the rest of your home. For instance, your home office could be one-half of a spare bedroom. For the most part, in order to be able to deduct expenses related to your home office, you must have a part of your home that you use exclusively and regularly either:

1) as your principal place of business, or
2) as a place to meet with your clients.

To determine whether your home office is your principal place of business, the IRS considers both the relative importance of the activities performed at your various places of business as well as the amount of time spent at each place where you conduct your business. Even if your home office isn't the location where you conduct most of your business, it will be treated as your principal place of business if you meet both of the following requirements:

1) You use it exclusively and regularly for administrative or management activities for your business
2) You have no other fixed location where you conduct substantial administrative or management activities for your business.

For example, if you are a self-employed electrician, most of your work will obviously be done on the clients' premises. However, as long as you do all of your administrative work in your home office, it will still qualify as your principal place of business. For reference, if you outsource some of your administrative activities (billing, for example), this will not disqualify you from meeting the above requirements.

There is one final thing to note regarding whether or not your home office qualifies for the deduction. The tax code says that the area must be used *exclusively* for business. So far, the IRS has held to a very literal definition of the word "exclusive." If you (or any family members) use the area in question for anything at all other than your business, it will disqualify you from taking the deduction. In other words, make sure that your kids are not playing in your office (on the computer, for instance) while you aren't home.

What Can Be Included

Generally, once you have determined that your home office qualifies for the deduction, you are allowed to deduct any expenses relating directly to the home office (as compared to relating to your entire home). Expenses that relate directly to your home office can be deducted in their entirety. These expenses would include things such as repairs on your office or repainting of the office.

You are also allowed to deduct a portion of the total expenses you incur in the operation of your home. This portion is simply a fraction calculated by dividing the square feet of your office by the square feet of your entire home. This category can include such expenses as:
- Homeowner's insurance
- Repairs and maintenance for your entire house.
- Cleaning supplies/services.
- Rent (if you rent your home)
- Deductible mortgage interest (if you own your home)
- Utilities

Depreciating Your Home

If you own your home, there is one final deduction that you can take for your home office: depreciation for your home. This works much like depreciating any other asset:
1) Determine the fair market value and the adjusted basis of your home. (The adjusted basis is generally what you paid for it.)
2) From the smaller of the two numbers, subtract the value of the land upon which your home is located. (A real estate appraiser can assess this value for you.)

3) Multiply the answer to #2 (known as the basis of the building) by the fraction you've been using for each of your home office deductions. Your answer is known as the business basis of the building.
4) The business basis of the building gets depreciated using a depreciation percentage each year as specified in the tax code. (The applicable percentages can be found in the instructions to Form 8829).

Should you choose to depreciate your home, be aware that there could be negative ramifications if/when you sell your home. As a result of depreciating a portion of your home, you will have a smaller adjusted cost basis when your home is sold. As such, the capital gain that you realize upon the sale of your home will be larger than it would have been had you not been depreciating it. That said, when most taxpayers sell their homes, they qualify for an exclusion that is large enough that it often nullifies the need to pay taxes on the capital gain. (Please see IRS Publication 523 for details on this exclusion.)

Is It Worth the Hassle?

Obviously, it takes some real time and effort to ensure that you are eligible for the home office deduction. You have to structure your day-to-day activities in a specific manner; you have additional records to keep; and you have to fill out a beast of a tax form (Form 8829). However, as you can see from all of the eligible expenses listed above, the deduction for business use of your home can be a very large one. Also, many of the expenses included in the deduction are ones that you are going to be paying one way or the other (homeowner's insurance, anyone?). As such, any amount you can save on your taxes from these expenses is pure money in your pocket.

Chapter 13 Simple Summary

- To qualify for the Home Office Deduction, you must use your home office *exclusively* and regularly as either your principal place of business or as a place to meet with clients.

- Even if you do not conduct the majority of your business from your home office, it will still qualify if you use it exclusively and regularly to conduct administrative or managerial functions for your business and there is no other fixed location where you conduct similar activities.

- As long as your home office qualifies, you can deduct all expenses related directly to the home office, and a portion of most expenses relating to your entire home. (The portion is calculated as the percentage of your entire home that is taken up by your home office.)

CHAPTER FOURTEEN

Saving for Retirement and Saving on Your Taxes

One of the single greatest parts of being self-employed is that there are more (and better) retirement plan options available to you than there are to most taxpayers. In addition to the standard traditional IRA/Roth IRA options that everybody has, you have three more options:

1) Simplified Employee Pension (SEP)
2) Savings Incentive Match Plan for Employees (a.k.a. SIMPLE IRA)
3) Qualified Plans (sometimes referred to as Keogh plans)

The bad news: Most of the IRS literature comparing these three options is particularly complicated.
The good news: Darned near all of that literature is irrelevant if you have no employees. If you have no employees, the primary difference between the plan options is simply the contribution limit for each. [Note: If you do have employees, and you want to set up a retirement plan for your business, it's strongly recommended that you get professional guidance.]

Retirement Plans in General

The basic idea behind each of your options is very similar to the idea behind a traditional IRA. That is, you get a tax deduction for each of the contributions you make to the plan, and your investments are allowed to grow tax-deferred until you start making withdrawals from the plan. Unfortunately, the deductions you receive for these contributions are not Schedule C deductions. They are, however, "above the line" deductions.

SEP IRAs

SEP IRAs work in almost the exact same way as a traditional IRA. That is, you are allowed an above the line deduction for any contributions you make. The only really important difference is the contribution limit. For 2007, if you have a SEP, you are allowed to contribute the lesser of:
  1) 25% of your net earnings from self-employment
  2) $45,000

Once the money is in the plan, you can invest it in all of the same things you would be allowed to invest in with a regular IRA (stocks, bonds, mutual funds, CDs, etc). Also, the same withdrawal rules apply. With a few exceptions, you cannot make withdrawals from the plan prior to age $59^{1/2}$ without being penalized.

One important thing to know is that, for purposes of calculating your maximum contribution, "net earnings from self-employment" is perhaps not quite what you'd expect. Basically, it's all your revenues, minus your expenses (makes sense so far), minus two other items:

1) The deduction for one-half of your self-employment tax.
2) The deductions for contributions to your SEP IRA.

Obviously, the idea of deducting your contribution amount when attempting to figure out how much you can contribute in the first place is a little confusing. Thankfully, the IRS gives you a cheat sheet to simplify the calculation. You can find it toward the end of IRS Publication 560.

SIMPLE IRAs

SIMPLE IRAs also function much like traditional IRAs. Again, the primary difference comes down to contribution limits. If you have a SIMPLE IRA, you can contribute (for 2007) 100% of your self-employment earnings up to $10,500 for people under 50, or $13,000 if you are 50 or over.

One other potentially important difference is that, should you have to make an early withdrawal from the plan within two years of the plan's inception date, you will be penalized more than you would be if it were a SEP IRA (25% penalty as compared to 10% penalty).

SEP vs. SIMPLE

As you've probably already noticed, SEP IRAs generally allow for a larger contribution than SIMPLE IRAs. The primary exception is for people whose business is a part-time business. More precisely, if you make less than $42,000 from your business, a SIMPLE IRA is going to allow for higher contributions than a SEP IRA.

Qualified Plans

The term "qualified plans" in this context encompasses several different types of plans. The four most common types are:

1) Profit-sharing plans
2) Money purchase plans
3) Solo 401(k) plans
4) Defined benefit plans.

Generally speaking, due to their lack of flexibility, profit-sharing plans and money purchase plans are not worth worrying about. Your needs can probably be met using a SEP IRA, SIMPLE IRA, Solo 401(k), or defined benefit plan.

Solo 401(k) Plans

A solo 401(k) plan functions very much like a 401(k) plan with a person's employer. The difference is that you are allowed to make a contribution in the role of employee *and* a contribution in the role of employer. You are allowed to contribute:

1) 100% of your earnings from self-employment, up to $15,500 for 2007 ($20,500 if you are 50 or over), plus
2) an employer contribution of 20% of your earnings from self-employment.

The total contribution is limited to the lesser of the taxpayer's earnings from self-employment, or (for 2007) $45,000. The only real downside to this type of plan is that it is generally more expensive to set up than a SEP IRA or a SIMPLE IRA.

Defined Benefit Plans

Defined benefit plans offer by far the largest potential for tax-deferred growth. The 2007 limit for a defined benefit plan contribution is the lesser of:

1) 100% of the participant's average self-employment earnings for his or her highest 3 consecutive calendar years, or
2) $180,000.

The downside to a defined benefit plan is an extreme lack of flexibility. When you set it up, you're required to determine a projected benefit (amount of income) that the plan will produce for you once you retire. Then, you are *required* to make contributions each year that will (according to current actuarial estimates) be able to provide the determined projected benefit.

As you might guess, due to the increased complexity involved, many investment firms will charge higher maintenance fees for a defined benefit plan than for any other type of retirement plan.

Pulling it All Together: How Things Work when You Have Multiple Plans

Given that you now have so many different options available to you, it's important to know how each of these plans interacts with other retirement accounts. Conveniently enough, none of the above-mentioned plans will affect your ability to contribute to a traditional IRA or a Roth IRA. Also, if you have a full-time job as an employee, and you are allowed to contribute to a 401(k), starting your own business-related retirement plan will not affect your eligibility to contribute to your 401(k) at work.

It is important to know that any contributions you make to your 401(k) (if you have one at work) or a business-related retirement plan will count toward your contribution limits for your business-related retirement plans. As an example, assume you make $40,000 from a full-time job, and $200,000 from your business. You have a 401(k) at work, and a SEP IRA for your business. Also, you are under 50 years old. Because $45,000 is less than 25% of your earnings from self-employment, your SEP IRA contribution limit is $45,000. However, if you contribute any money to your 401(k) at work, the amount you contribute is deducted from your maximum contribution to your SEP. So if you contributed $4,000 to your 401(k), you could only contribute $41,000 to your SEP IRA.

Given that having multiple plans doesn't increase your maximum contribution amount, it generally makes sense to only have one retirement plan for your business. However, if you also have a "real job" that offers a matching contribution, be sure to at least make sufficient contributions to get the maximum match. Generally you want to make your decision in order to maximize your potential contributions, while still keeping in mind the fees that would be associated with each type of plan at your favorite investment firm/bank.

Chapter 14 Simple Summary

- As a business owner, you have several options for retirement plans. In most cases, contributions to these plans count as above the line deductions.

- Generally speaking, you want to choose the plan that has the highest contribution limit for your situation.

- Due to their simplicity, SEP IRAs and SIMPLE IRAs are often excellent options. If your self-employment earnings are under $42,000, you will be able to contribute more to a SIMPLE. Earn above $42,000, and you will be able to contribute more to a SEP.

- Solo 401(k) plans and defined benefit plans can allow for very large contributions, but they are likely to be accompanied by higher set-up and maintenance costs from your bank or investment firm.

PART THREE

The Big Question: Which Business Structure Should I Choose?

The Significance of Business Structure

Probably the most frequently asked question by all business owners (or future business owners) is, "What type of legal structure should I have for my business?" Of course, the answer is not often easy to determine. You're most likely a sole proprietor or LLC owner at the moment, otherwise you probably wouldn't be reading this guide. From time to time, however, it's a good practice to reevaluate your current structure to see if it still meets your needs.

Your answer to this question will impact several facets of your business. The way the Federal government taxes your business will be defined by your business structure. The way your state (and other states too, if you have clients in other states) taxes your business will be defined by your business structure. Countless legal issues will be impacted by your business structure. You get the idea. As such, this is a question worthy of a great deal of thought.

You want to make sure to choose a structure that fits your business now, but you also need to take into account where you see your business in 5, 10, or 20 years. But don't worry. If you later decide that your current structure is no longer a good fit, it's possible (and sometimes not very difficult) to make a switch. So, let's take a look at your options...

CHAPTER FIFTEEN

Sole Proprietorship: A Wonderful Place to Start

By far the most popular legal structure, sole proprietorship offers much in the way of convenience and simplicity. Forming a sole proprietorship generally costs significantly less and takes significantly less time than any of the other options. Legal issues are much more straightforward, and there are far fewer complex tax issues. It's no surprise that over 80% of businesses in the United States are sole proprietorships.

All You Have to Do Is...

One of the largest benefits of doing business as a sole proprietorship is how easy it is to form one. The most difficult thing you will have to do is find out which business licenses your city/county/state require you to have, and then apply for them. This isn't terribly difficult to do, and it generally doesn't cost a great deal. (At least, it doesn't cost very much when compared to the attorney's fees you would likely end up paying if you were forming a corporation, for instance.) For reference, some helpful resources for forming your business entity, sole proprietorship or otherwise, can be found in the appendix.

If you decide that your business is going to have a name other than your own personal name, your state or county will probably require you to file a "Doing Business As" registration. The requirements may vary based upon your location, so be sure to check into this, as you certainly don't want to pay for it if you don't have to.

Another aspect of the simplicity of being a sole proprietor is that, unless you plan on having employees, you will not be required to obtain a Federal Employer Identification Number (the rough equivalent of a Social Security Number, but for a business).

Pass-Through Entities: Why Your Business Doesn't Exist as far as the IRS is Concerned

Sole proprietorships (along with partnerships, and some LLCs) are known as "pass-through entities" for Federal income tax purposes. What this means is that the income from your business is simply "passed through" to your own personal income tax return. This makes for a comparatively simple situation when April 15 comes around.

For purposes of clarification, let's compare this situation to the situation of a corporation. Corporations are taxable entities for Federal income taxes. As such, a corporation will have to file its own separate income tax return, and it will be taxed on its income/profits (similar to the way individuals are taxed). Then, when the business's profits are paid out to its owners (in a payment known as a dividend), the owners are taxed on the dividend income. In effect, this causes a corporation's profits to be subject to double taxation.

The Danger of Unlimited Liability

The single biggest downfall of doing business as a sole proprietor is probably the concept of "unlimited liability." What this term refers to is the fact that, for legal purposes, there is no distinction between your personal assets and the assets of your business. So? Why does that matter? It will matter in two types of scenarios: Business debt, and business lawsuits.

Let's say that you run a retail store, and you decide to take out a $250,000 bank loan in the name of your business with the idea of opening a new location. Unfortunately, things don't go as planned, and your business eventually goes belly-up before you can repay the loan. Because of your unlimited liability, your bank can now come after you personally (and pretty much anything you own) for the $250,000. Scary, huh?

Let's use an example to explain the lawsuit scenario as well. Imagine you have a business making and installing porch swings. You install a swing at the home of an elderly couple. Three days later, the chain breaks, and your customer lands on her porch, breaking her hip, ankle, and wrist in the process. Think she might sue? If she ends up winning the lawsuit, she'd be allowed to come after your personal assets, just like the bank can in the other example.

Now, before you panic, spend a little time thinking about the specifics of your business. If you plan to take the slow-but-steady route rather than taking out any loans for your business, suddenly unlimited liability is a bit less of an issue. Now, think about the nature of your product or service. Is it one that is at all likely to create any lawsuits? Perhaps a modest professional liability insurance policy would be the most efficient/affordable way to protect yourself.

Chapter 15 Simple Summary

- Doing business as a sole proprietor makes for by far the simplest tax situation when it comes to legal structures for your business.

- Sole proprietorships are referred to as pass-through entities, meaning that income from the business is simply reported on the owner's personal Form 1040.

- The downside to running a sole proprietorship is that you have unlimited liability for the debts of the business. Depending upon your business, this can make for a dangerous situation.

CHAPTER SIXTEEN

Partnerships
(Because You Can't Call it a *Sole* Proprietorship Anymore Once There Are Two People Involved)

If a person simply decides one day to start a business, by default, he will be running a sole proprietorship. If two or more people simply decide one day to start a business, by default, they'll be running a partnership. As we'll soon see, partnerships function similarly to sole proprietorships in many ways.

Pass-Through Tax Treatment

Just like a sole proprietorship, partnerships are pass-through entities. In other words, the partnership itself is not subject to a tax on its income. Instead, its income is allocated to the partners, and they each pay tax on their portion. Partnerships are required to file a Form 1065, on which the revenues and expenses for the partnership are listed, and the partnership's profit is calculated. Accompanying the Form 1065 is a Schedule K-1 for each partner. These schedules serve the purpose of allocating the partnership's profit or loss to the various partners. Each partner then reports her share of the profit/loss on her personal Form 1040. Allocations of the partnership's profit, like income from a sole proprietorship, are subject to the self-employment tax.

One particular issue that complicates matters is the fact that partners are taxed based upon the amount of income they are allocated, regardless of how much income is actually distributed to them. For example, let's say Edward and Brad form a partnership, and earn $50,000 profit in the first year of operation. They decide to pay out $15,000 to each partner, and use the remaining $20,000 to grow their new business. Even though each partner only received $15,000 in cash from the partnership, he will be taxed upon $25,000 of income (half of the partnership's profit). The situation isn't quite as bad as that makes it sound, however. Should the partners later decide that they want to pay out that $20,000 that they had originally reinvested in the business, the payment to the owners won't be taxed. [Note: this is a very simplified explanation of the rather complicated topic known as "basis" as it applies to a partnership. If you need more in-depth information about basis, take a look at IRS Publication 541, at http://www.irs.gov/publications/p541/index.html.]

Unlimited Liability—Even for Each Other!

Another way in which partnerships are similar to sole proprietorships is the issue of unlimited liability. The only difference here is that it's even scarier than if you work alone. Let's say you and your neighbor form a partnership, and to get the business started, you take out a loan for $70,000. If the business fails, the creditor has the option of coming after *either* partner. For the whole thing! Granted, if the bank successfully sues you for the money, you will, in turn, be able to sue your neighbor for his share of the debt. But you'll certainly be incurring court costs and attorney's fees, and quite likely waiting a pretty good while before you get your cash.

Quite in fact, a plaintiff can sue any of the partners for a debt, even if the debt arose from a malpractice suit, which resulted from the malpractice of only one of the partners. For example, assume Jack and Jill form a partnership for their chiropractic practice. Jack then accidentally injures a client's spinal cord during a session. When the client sues, if the business itself does not have sufficient funds to cover the debt, the client can sue either partner (or both partners) for the remainder, regardless of the fact that Jill had nothing to do with the injury.

Limited Partnerships

In the discussion above, every time the term "partnership" was used, a more precise term would have been "general partnership." Unless there is a clause in the Partnership Agreement clearly stating otherwise, all partnerships are general partnerships. The other option is to form a limited partnership.

In a limited partnership there are two types of partners: general partners and limited partners. General partners are subject to all the rules mentioned above in terms of unlimited liability. Limited partners, on the other hand, have limited liability. They can only lose the amount of money that they invest in the partnership; they cannot be sued for any of the partnership's obligations/debts. Limited partnerships can have as many limited partners as they choose, but are required to have at least one general partner.

Forming a limited partnership may seem like a great way to protect most of the partners. There is one large catch though. Limited partners are *not* allowed to participate in the management or day-to-day operations of the partnership. If they do, they will lose their limited liability status.

Chapter 16 Simple Summary

- Like sole proprietorships, partnerships are easy to form, and they offer a pass-through tax scenario in which the income from the business is simply passed through to the owners and reported on their respective Form 1040s.

- Also like sole proprietorships, partnerships do not offer limited liability protection. This can be particularly dangerous in that each partner can be held personally liable for debts caused entirely by the other partner's actions.

- Limited partnerships (in contrast to the general partnership structure, frequently simply referred to as a "partnership") do offer a degree of limited liability. Limited partners can only lose the money that they invested, no more. However, they cannot participate in the management or daily operations of the partnership.

CHAPTER SEVENTEEN

LLCs—Limited Liability Companies

Ubiquitous: Being or seeming to be everywhere at the same time; omnipresent (American Heritage Dictionary, Fourth Edition).

Just about anything you read these days regarding different business structures will end up recommending that you form an LLC, almost regardless of your location, type of business, or business goals. Forming an LLC may not be a bad idea, but it might not be the best option either.

A Little Background

Part of the reason that LLCs are practically always the legal structure that ends up being recommended by most advisors/writers is that the LLC was, quite in fact, created with the explicit purpose of combining the best parts of all the other business structure options. LLCs are created under state law, not Federal law. As such, depending upon where your business operates, the specifics will vary (more on this later).

Limited Liability

One of the principal goals behind the creation of the LLC was to create an easy-to-form business entity that would allow for the protection of limited liability. That's why LLC members (owners) are generally not held liable for the obligations of the business. If the business is sued for an outstanding debt, none of the owners can be held personally liable. Well, that's the idea anyway. It isn't always so simple, though, as we'll soon see.

In some states, the limited liability from LLCs applies not just to the business debt, but to business lawsuits as well. For example, let's say you and a business acquaintance form a tax preparation business, and together you form an LLC. Then one busy day during tax season, your partner makes a terrible mistake on a client's return, which ends up costing the client thousands of dollars in penalties. Don't worry. (At least not too much.) The client will not be able to come after your personal assets. Such is the benefit of having an LLC. Unfortunately, as we'll soon see, your partner may not be so lucky.

Again, LLC law varies from state to state, so be *sure* to check your state law before assuming you have this protection.

Federal Tax Treatment

For Federal tax purposes, LLCs are disregarded entities. That is, the IRS will treat your business as if the LLC had never been formed. As such, if you are the sole owner of the LLC (known as a single-member LLC), it will be taxed as if it were a sole proprietorship. In other words, you'll be filling out a Schedule C, Schedule SE, etc. (By the way, the just-stated fact is the reason that this guide holds itself out to be a guide for both sole proprietors and LLC owners.) If the LLC has multiple owners (a multiple-member LLC), it will be taxed as a general partnership. That means you'll fill out Form 1065, Schedule K-1, etc.

This tax treatment is one of the main benefits of forming an LLC. Why is this a benefit? Because the tax considerations involved in owning a sole proprietorship are far, far simpler than the tax consequences involved in personally owning a corporation.

Another benefit of owning an LLC is that, should the owner eventually find himself in a situation where it would be more beneficial to be taxed as a corporation than as a sole proprietorship, he has that option. By filing Form 8832 with the IRS, an LLC owner can elect to have his LLC taxed as a corporation. No need to actually incorporate.

So When Would Somebody *Not* Want to Form an LLC?

So far, everything about LLCs sounds pretty good I imagine. And that's the point. That's why the LLC is the structure *du jour* in the small business community. There are, however, some factors that might sway your decision in a different direction.

First, let's discuss state taxes. While the LLC leaves the business owner in a nice situation for Federal taxes, the same isn't necessarily true of state taxes. Some states (Illinois, California, and Rhode Island for instance) have chosen to impose an entity-level tax on the LLC, rather than treating it like a sole proprietorship. Obviously this creates a rather complex situation (read as: very lucrative for your accountant/tax preparer) in that you'll have a sole proprietorship according to the IRS and a somewhat-like-a-corporation business according to your state's Department of Revenue.

Other states have their own unique rules. New York for example treats the LLC the same way the Federal government does, but also imposes a tax based upon the number of owners of the LLC.

More Reasons an LLC Might Not be Your Best Bet

In addition to the potential complication of state taxes, there is an even larger issue to consider. Remember the whole bit about LLCs granting limited liability? It's not exactly a steadfast rule. For instance, it doesn't apply when the lawsuit arises from services that you performed personally.

Imagine that you've gone into business as an electrician and formed an LLC. Then one day shortly after doing some work on a client's residence, the home catches fire and is severely damaged. The fire investigators end up declaring that faulty electrical wiring was the cause of the fire. You're going to be facing a lawsuit, and because you performed the services personally, you will not have the benefit of limited liability. In other words, the plaintiff will be able to sue you for both your business and personal assets.

So at least the LLC structure will still protect you from creditors being able to come after your personal assets as a result of the business's debts, yes? Well, maybe. If you need to take out a loan for your business, and the business is still rather new, it's a near-certainty that your bank is going to require you to personally guarantee the loan. As such, your LLC isn't going to help you one bit. (It doesn't make the situation any worse; it's just not going to help.)

Chapter 17 Simple Summary

- LLCs can sometimes be the best of both worlds. LLCs provide pass-through tax treatment, and (to an extent) limited liability.

- Before forming an LLC, be sure to check how LLCs are taxed in your state, as some state laws can make for a rather complicated tax situation for your business.

- While LLCs generally provide limited liability, you won't be protected in the case of a lawsuit arising as a direct result of services you performed personally.

CHAPTER EIGHTEEN

Corporations, a.k.a. "C Corps"

The original method for achieving limited liability was to form a corporation. In contrast to the relative novelty of the LLC, corporations have been around for centuries. (Corporations, then known as "joint-stock companies," played a major role in the colonization of the Americas.)

A Distinct Legal Entity

What has made corporations so useful over the years is their unique legal status. Legally, a corporation is a distinct entity. In other words, a corporation has basically the same rights and responsibilities that a regular citizen has. It can sue and be sued. It can buy and sell property. It can enter into a contract. And, like all of us, it has to pay taxes.

What this means for you, should you incorporate your business, is that you'll get to enjoy the benefit of limited liability. However, your limited liability will be subject to effectively the same exceptions as discussed earlier regarding LLCs.

Big Plans? Incorporating Might Be the Answer

If your business plan involves attracting a large amount of capital from other investors, forming a corporation is very possibly your only option. Many investors will not even consider investing in your business unless they are given the limited liability offered by a corporate structure.

When you incorporate, ownership of your business is broken down into shares. (The number of shares issued will be stated in your articles of incorporation, but it is a more or less arbitrary number.) At first, assuming you are still the sole owner, you will own 100% of the shares. You are then allowed to sell any number of them you choose, at any price agreeable to both yourself and the investor.

Each share of stock entitles the owner to a share in the profits of the company. Also, each share entitles the holder to one vote anytime a major decision is being made. Because of the voting power accompanying the stock, there is obviously a large benefit to retaining greater than 50% of the shares in the company.

That said, if you're working with major investors, there is a good chance that they will require you to give up majority ownership in your company. In this situation, you would still be in charge of the day-to-day operations (as the President/CEO of the company), but the majority owners would have the final say in all the major decisions (including naming a new CEO, should they decide to).

Tax Treatment of Corporations

The tax treatment of a corporation is right in line with the idea that a corporation is its own entity. More specifically, corporations have to pay income tax on their profits. The income tax system for corporations is very similar to that for individuals. For instance, they are entitled to deductions for their business expenses, the same way you are for your LLC or sole proprietorship.

There are, however, several differences. For example, the tax brackets for corporations are completely different. The tax brackets for corporations (to be contrasted with those for individuals, shown on p. 32) are as follows:

Tax Rates for Corporations	
$0-$50,000	15%
$50,001-$75,000	25%
$75,001-$100,000	34%
$100,001-$335,000	39%
$335,001-$10,000,000	34%
$10,000,001-$15,000,000	35%
$15,000,001-$18,333,333	38%
Over $18,333,333	35%

Also, corporations only have one type of deduction: business deductions. As such, there is no need to distinguish between above the line, below the line, etc.

Dividends

After a corporation pays taxes on its profits, it has the option of either paying them out to the owners (shareholders) or reinvesting them in the business. When corporate profits are paid out to shareholders, the payment is known as a dividend.

Dividends are taxable income to shareholders. Historically, they have been taxed at the taxpayer's highest tax bracket. However, the Jobs and Growth Tax Relief Reconciliation Act of 2003 temporarily reduced the maximum tax rate on dividends to 15%. This lower rate was originally scheduled to expire in 2008, but has been extended through 2010. The fact that dividends are taxable to shareholders means that corporate profits are, in effect, doubly taxed unless they are reinvested in the business.

Paying Yourself a Salary

The alternative method for getting money out of your corporation and into your personal bank account is to pay yourself a salary. Your corporation will get a deduction for the amount of salary it pays you.

As such, if you paid out the entire amount that would—if weren't paying yourself a salary—be your business's profits, the net tax result will be basically the same as if you had a sole proprietorship. In other words, you will be paying income taxes according to the tax brackets for individuals (the income will simply be salary as compared to self-employment income). And you will be paying the same amount for social security and Medicare taxes. The only difference being that, instead of paying them all personally in the form of SE Tax, your corporation will be responsible for half the bill, and you will be responsible for half the bill.

When a Single-Owner C Corp Makes Sense: Income Splitting Explained

Even if you have no intentions of attracting outside investors, there is one primary situation in which forming a C corp. (or an LLC taxable as a C corp.) makes sense. That situation arises when you find that your business is producing more money than you need to pay your bills, and you realize that you can afford to reinvest a large portion of the profits back into the business.

In short, the idea is to split up your total business income so that some of it is taxable to you personally (as salary) and some of it is taxable as net income to your corporation. The goal is to pay less tax overall than would be paid if the entire income was allocated either to yourself or to the corporation.

For instance, let's assume that you are single and you own a business with net income of $100,000. If you were a sole proprietor, that would put you in the 28% tax bracket, and all $100,000 of the income would be subject to the 15.3% SE tax as well.

Now imagine your business is a corporation. You pay out $50,000 in salary, and retain the other $50,000 in the business in order to fund its growth. With $50,000 in net income, your business never gets above the 15% tax bracket. And with $50,000 personal income, you only make it to the 25% tax bracket. And only the $50,000 in salary ends up being subject to the 15.3% social security and Medicare taxes. That's a lot of tax savings.

Before attempting this strategy, be sure to consult a professional tax advisor. While income splitting is often an excellent means to save on taxes, the tax code now has several provisions built-in, which allow the IRS to disregard a corporation (that is, treat it as a pass-through entity) should they conclude that the corporation was formed solely to avoid paying taxes.

Chapter 18 Simple Summary

- C corporations function legally as if they were actual people. They can sign contracts, borrow money, loan money, sue, be sued, and so on.

- The level of limited liability provided by forming a C corporation is generally regarded as the best, though it is still not perfect.

- Income earned by a C corporation and then passed on to shareholders is referred to as a dividend. Such distributions are subject to two levels of tax: the corporation is taxed for the income earned, and then the shareholders are taxed for the money they receive as dividends.

- If you do not plan to distribute all of your business income to yourself, but rather, you plan to reinvest a substantial portion of it into the business, forming a C corp. can save you money on taxes by allowing for income splitting strategies.

- If you intend to raise capital from a large amount of investors, forming a C corp. is going to be your only option for the most part.

CHAPTER NINETEEN

S Corps: Outdated?

An S corporation is simply a regular corporation that has made an election (on Form 2553) to be taxed as a pass-through entity. The original idea was to offer both the limited liability of a corporation as well as the potential tax benefits of single-level taxation (as compared to the double taxation of the C corp. structure).

However, forming an LLC can offer both of these benefits with far less organizational/legal costs to set up the business. Also, the tax situation of an S corp. is generally far more complicated than that of a pass-through LLC. As such, many experts expect to see a decline in the rate of S corp. formations over the coming years. That said, there is still one primary tax benefit of having an S corp. over an LLC.

No SE Tax on Business Profits for S Corps

The single remaining benefit of forming an S corp. as compared to an LLC is that S corp. owners do not have to pay SE tax for business profits. Sound good? It is, but probably not *quite* as good as you're thinking.

If they provide a substantial amount of services for the business, S corp. owners are required to pay themselves a "reasonable" salary. What this means is that, assuming you're still going to be running your business, you have to pay yourself a salary. And that salary is going to be subject to social security and Medicare taxes (paid 50% by you personally and 50% by the S corp.), which will be equal to what the self-employment tax would have been had you never incorporated and remained a sole proprietor. No tax savings so far.

However, let's say your business revenues exceed expenses by $70,000. You could quite possibly make the case that $50,000 would be a reasonable salary. If you did that, only $50,000 would be subject to social security and Medicare taxes. You could then pay out the remaining $20,000 to yourself as a distribution of business profits, not subject to the SE tax.

Eligibility for S Corp Election

In order to be eligible to make the S corp. election, a corporation must meet all of the following requirements:
1) It must be a domestic corporation.
2) It must have no more than 100 shareholders.
3) The shareholders can only be individuals, estates, and exempt organizations. (In other words, no corporations as shareholders.)
4) It can have no nonresident alien shareholders.
5) It can have only one class of stock (disregarding differences in voting rights).
6) It cannot be a bank or insurance company.
7) All shareholders must consent to the election.

The Downside to S Corps

S corps are an accountant's dream (read as: lots of billable hours). The reason is that they come with a far greater amount of complexity than a typical pass-through entity. First, there is the issue of making sure that what you are paying yourself as salary is, in fact, defensibly reasonable. Next, you must always be careful to avoid falling into any of the above situations, which would render your business ineligible for S corp. status (thus, forcing C corp. status on you, whether you like it or not).

In fact, there are several more accounting/tax issues relating to S corps that we haven't even touched on. So before running out and forming an S corp. in order to save on self-employment taxes, be sure to do a cost/benefit analysis weighing the tax savings against the additional required billing from your attorney and accountant.

Chapter 19 Simple Summary

- Like C corporations, S corporations count as legal entities, with substantially all the same rights and responsibilities that individuals have.

- In contrast to regular corporations, S corporations are pass-through entities.

- The unique benefit of forming an S corp. is that distributions of business profits (after paying yourself the required "reasonable" salary) are not subject to SE taxes.

- While forming an S corp. may save you money on taxes, it will certainly cost you more money every year by necessitating a great deal more legal and accounting advice.

CONCLUSION

When to Try and Tackle All this Yourself, and When to Get Professional Assistance

Even with your new knowledge of the various tax issues that you're faced with as a business owner, you have to decide whether you intend to actually file your own taxes, or if you want professional assistance. Obviously, the factors in this decision are both financial and personal. (Is anything relating to your finances *not* personal?)

To make the decision easier, let's first assume that you could do the job as well as a professional (i.e., you could do just as good of a job maximizing your deductions, credits, etc). In this case, it pretty much comes down to how long it would take you. Let's say it would take you ten hours. Just compare the income you could make in ten hours marketing to clients and prospects to the cost of having a professional do your taxes for you.

Next, you have to actually assess whether or not you think a professional would be likely to be able to find ways to lower your taxes that you wouldn't be able to find. Deduct this amount of tax savings from the cost of the professional. (This is, of course, an absolute guess.)

Finally, and perhaps most importantly, ask yourself whether or not you think it would be a fun exercise to do your own taxes. You probably already know the answer, but if not, go ahead and give it a try once. Just remember that if you get sufficiently frustrated, it's OK to go back to running the business you enjoy, and pass the tax-related work off to a professional.

Helpful Resources

Useful Links

http://www.irs.gov/formspubs/index.html?portlet=3
> The IRS's page for downloading Forms and Publications.

www.pipertax.com
> Piper Tax Group's website. Includes tax FAQs, tax articles, and other useful links.

www.taxalmanac.org
> An excellent compendium of tax research resources, including a wonderful discussion board.

www.mycorporation.com
> Run by Intuit®, the creators of TurboTax® this site offers what I can best describe as entity-creation services. They can help you with filing a DBA for a sole proprietorship, help with forming an LLC, or even help should you decide upon incorporating.

www.quickbooks.com and www.quicken.com
> Also run by Intuit, these two programs are excellent bookkeeping resources. QuickBooks® is generally what I'd recommend, but if you want a more simplified version, go with Quicken®.

www.nolo.com
> The most well known (and deservedly so) publisher of legal self-help books. Useful for everybody; essential for business owners.

www.sba.gov
> Home of the U.S. Small Business Administration. Here you can find any number of resources from links to local business licensing agencies to articles about how to find investors for your business.

www.uspto.gov
> United States Patent and Trademark Office.

IRS Publications

Publication 334 – Tax guide for small businesses.

Publication 535 – Business expenses.

Publication 463 – Travel, entertainment, gift, and car expenses.

Publication 587 – Business use of your home.

Publication 946 – How to depreciate property.

Publication 505 – Tax withholding and estimated tax.

Recommended Reading

Start Late, Finish Rich: A No-Fail Plan for Achieving Financial Freedom at Any Age, by David Bach

Instant Income, by Janet Switzer

From Entrepreneur to Infopreneur: Make Money with Books, E-books, and Information Products, by Stephanie Chandler

Aiming at Amazon: The NEW Business of Self Publishing, by Aaron Shepard

How to Run a Thriving Business: Strategies for Success and Satisfaction, by Ralph Warner

Home-Based Business for Dummies, by Paul and Sarah Edwards and Peter Economy

Thinking Like an Entrepreneur: How to Make Intelligent Business Decisions That Will Lead to Success in Building and Growing Your Own Company, by Peter Hupalo

Printed in the United States
94210LV00006B/291/A

9 780615 158433